Test Your Cat

HarperCollins*Publishers*
1 London Bridge Street
London SE1 9GF

www.harpercollins.co.uk

First published in Great Britain by
Angus & Robertson (UK) as *The Cat Intelligence Test* 1982
This edition published by HarperCollins*Publishers* 2017

48

Text © E.M. Bard 1980
Illustrations © Doubleday & Company, Inc. 1980
Illustrations by Robert Leydenfrost
Interior design: Rosamund Saunders
Cover images © Shutterstock

A catalogue record for this book is available from the British Library

ISBN 978-0-00-255502-9

Printed and bound by CPI Group (UK) Ltd, Croydon, CR0 4YY

MIX
Paper from
responsible sources
FSC™ C007454

This book is produced from independently certified FSC™ paper
to ensure responsible forest management.

For more information visit: www.harpercollins.co.uk/green

Test Your Cat

THE CAT IQ TEST

E.M.BARD

DRAWINGS BY ROBERT LEYDENFROST

HarperCollins*Publishers*

Foreword

Is your cat a genius? I'm pretty sure mine is.

I am a champion of the intelligence of cats. Being a cat lover, and having lived with cats all my life I feel strongly that their perception, brilliance and comprehension should not be underestimated. The way my gorgeous cat, Lady, looks at me sometimes makes me feel that I need an IQ test, not her! She outsmarts me on most things, sourcing food, opening doors so she doesn't have to exert herself with the cat flap, sleeping on my favourite cashmere blanket – the list goes on!

Even if you don't think your cat is quite ready for Mastermind, this fun quiz, based on credited cat intelligence tests, is a fun way to discover if your beloved pet is the feline equivalent to Einstein. It's also an enjoyable way to bond with your cat. As with people, cats have very diverse personalities and they are fascinating when you really take time to get to know them.

When I first wrote about my fictional cat, Alfie, he was a character based on a mixture of many cats I have had the pleasure to live with throughout my life. He is an incredibly clever, perceptive, loyal, problem-solving cat, but the number of people who have been in touch with me to tell me that he reminds them of their cat has taken me by surprise. Alfie has a little bit of an ego though, so if I tried to get him to take this test he would possibly look at me with disdain and convey to me 'I do not need to take such a test, everyone knows I'm a genius.' I can almost hear him saying that!

This book is the perfect gift for any cat lover, it's amusing and entertaining, but actually it makes perfect sense, because not only does it test your cat, but it also tests you as an owner as to how well you know your perfect pet. However well your cat scores on the genius scale, it will definitely strengthen your relationship.

Rachel Wells
Author of *Alfie the Doorstep Cat*

Contents

Introduction

Anyone who has ever owned a cat has at one time or another been amazed at his pet's natural abilities and wisdom. At times, cats and kittens seem to thrive on entertaining their owners with cute tricks and unusual behaviour. In actuality, the cantankerous and often irrepressible behaviour is an important part of their intellectual development.

Cats develop their learning and understanding ability according to their background, their experiences, their age and their living conditions. Your pet may be around conditions that make him* nervous or upset. He may be around conditions that make him relaxed and lazy. Sometimes, when they are bothered, cats try to run and hide. Sometimes they will attempt to fight or outsmart whatever is bothering them. The way in which your pet responds to his living conditions is an indication of his learning and understanding ability – or, simply put, his intelligence.

The Cat IQ Test measures the overall intellectual development of your cat. There are four areas of development that, when taken together, make up your cat's intelligence:

* 'Him' is used throughout as the neuter pronoun, and of course includes 'her' as well.

1. Co-ordination Skills

This includes the use of small and large muscles, how your cat moves and balances, his reflex actions, body sensitivity and control, and his preference for using one side of his body over another.

2. Communication Skills

This area of cat development deals with the pet's ability to make himself understood or to get attention. Cats are able to gain attention by using both their voices and their bodies. Communication skills measured here include voice level and intensity, and your cat's ability to understand directions.

3. Reasoning Ability

This is perhaps the most difficult area to measure. It involves testing how your cat solves the various problems he encounters and how he adjusts to his surroundings. Your cat's alertness, concentration and reactions to dangerous situations are also measured.

4. Social Behaviour

This includes a wide range of both personal and social skills that are developed and used by your cat. The way in which your cat gets along with you, other people and other animals is an important indication of your cat's overall intelligence.

The Cat IQ Test is divided into four sections, three of which involve observing your cat in a variety of usual situations. After you have carefully watched your cat in these situations a number of times, you should mark down how he behaved, either where provided for in each section or on the scorecard on page 125.

Section B of the test is an administered test. For this section, you perform certain activities with your cat and mark down your cat's response. Since the cat must actively participate in the test to score well in this section, it is important that you provide him with the specific testing items mentioned in the directions to that section. You'll find that they are common objects. Also, you should only administer this section of the test when your cat is calm and co-operative. (The test may, of course, be discontinued at any time, and started over later.)

The Cat IQ Test may be used for all cats or kittens. It is recommended that the pet be at least eight weeks old before the test is attempted. Although the test may be given more than once, a one-day waiting period is suggested in order to avoid the practice effect often found in a re-testing situation. Careful administration of the test is necessary in order to obtain a good estimate of the pet's intellectual abilities. Do not teach your cat the correct responses. The goal of this test is to observe and record the total way in which your pet has been able to adjust to his surroundings. By using several of the major areas of pet development to judge the cat's learning and understanding skills, you will be obtaining his overall intellectual level. No pre-coaching or remedial drill may be provided before the test is given. When testing handicapped cats, special provisions need to be made. If the pet has a visual or hearing problem, award the pet credit for items he is unable to attempt due to his learning disability. Physically disabling conditions should be handled in the same manner.

After you have done all the testing and have determined your cat's final score, you can compare his score to that of other cats in general, or to those of your cat's type, sex or age. Of course, keep in mind that intelligence is only one facet of your cat's unique personality. Some wonderful pets may score poorly on this test because of limited experience or unusual backgrounds. This book provides specific suggestions for improving your cat's intelligence and sociability.

But for now, you're ready to begin.

THE CAT IQ TEST

Section A: Cat Observation Test

Directions

Read each of the test questions carefully. Rate your pet according to the scale below. Before rating your cat, observe him in a variety of situations and at different times. This will provide a more accurate measure.

Rating Scale

The following scale should be referred to when scoring your pet's behaviour:

Category	Rating Points
Never	1
Seldom	2
Often	3
Usually	4
Always	5

Recording

Tick the appropriate box and write the score on the line following the test item or on the scorecard on page 125. This will be the number of points your pet receives for each item.

Scoring

At the end of Section A, add up the total number of points earned.

I

Eats or requests food on a regular schedule

(e.g. desire for food can be predicted, eats around the same time each day).

Never: ☐ 1 point

Seldom: ☐ 2 points

Often: ☐ 3 points

Usually: ☑ 4 points

Always: ☐ 5 points

Points Received: 4

2

Enjoys a variety of foods

(e.g. both pet food and people food).

Never: ☐ 1 point

Seldom: ☑ 2 points

Often: ☐ 3 points

Usually: ☐ 4 points

Always: ☐ 5 points

Points Received: 2

3

Is able to show displeasure with food he is given

(e.g. turns dish over, uses dish for litter box).

Never: ☐ 1 point

Seldom: ☐ 2 points

Often: ☑ 3 points

Usually: ☐ 4 points

Always: ☐ 5 points

Points Received: 3 ....

4

Cleans face after eating

(e.g. wipes whiskers or mouth with tongue or paws).

Never: ☐ 1 point

Seldom: ☐ 2 points

Often: ☐ 3 points

Usually: ☑ 4 points

Always: ☐ 5 points

Points Received: ...4...........

5

Keeps tail flat on floor when eating

(tail touches floor behind or to side of pet).

Never: ☐ 1 point

Seldom: ☐ 2 points

Often: ☑ 3 points

Usually: ☑ 4 points

Always: ☒ 5 points

Points Received: ...54.........

6

Is able to get the attention of people around him when he wants

(e.g. by rubbing, clawing, purring, crying).

Never: ☐ 1 point

Seldom: ☐ 2 points

Often: ☐ 3 points

Usually: ☐ 4 points

Always: ☑ 5 points

Points Received: ......5........

7

Recognises sounds

that precede his feeding

(e.g. can opener, refrigerator door, food wrapper).

Never: ☐ 1 point

Seldom: ☑ 2 points

Often: ☐ 3 points

Usually: ☐ 4 points

Always: ☐ 5 points

Points Received: 2 ....

8

Sleeps in the same place each night.

Never: ☐ 1 point

Seldom: ☐ 2 points

Often: ☐ 3 points

Usually: ☑ 4 points

Always: ☐ 5 points

Points Received: ....4........

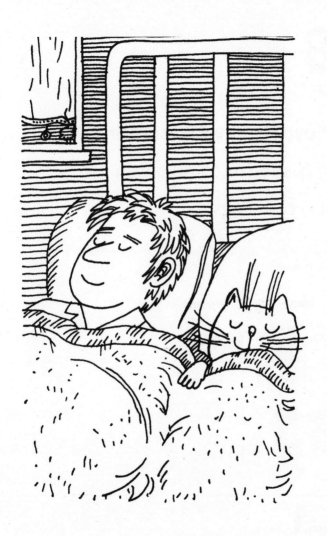

9

Moves ears while sleeping in response to noises in his surroundings

(e.g. phone, doorbell, water running, door closing, voices, wind, rain).

Never: ☐ 1 point

Seldom: ☐ 2 points

Often: ☑ 3 points

Usually: ☐ 4 points

Always: ☐ 5 points

Points Received: 3

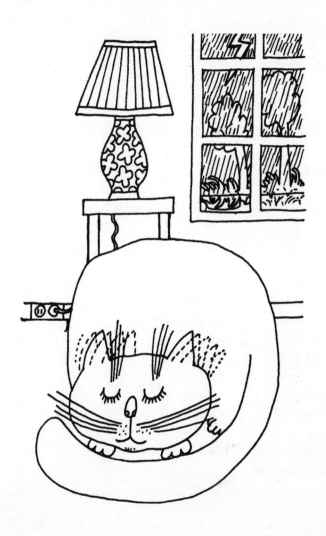

10

Has regularly established sleeping patterns

(goes to sleep and gets up around the same times each day).

Never: ☐ 1 point

Seldom: ☑ 2 points

Often: ☐ 3 points

Usually: ☐ 4 points

Always: ☐ 5 points

Points Received: 2 ....

11

Watches movement around him

(e.g. sits by window, observes other animals, is sensitive to small movements).

Never: ☐ 1 point

Seldom: ☐ 2 points

Often: ☐ 3 points

Usually: ☑ 4 points

Always: ☐ 5 points

Points Received: ....4........

12

Reveals his mood through the position or state of his tail

(e.g. bushy, hidden, wrapped around legs, curled around body, straight up in air, limp or relaxed).

Never: ☒ 1 point

Seldom: ☐ 2 points

Often: ☐ 3 points

Usually: ☐ 4 points

Always: ☑ 5 points

Points Received: 5 ....

13

Is able to remain totally still, while awake, for a minimum of two minutes.

Never: ☐ 1 point

Seldom: ☐ 2 points

Often: ☑ 3 points

Usually: ☐ 4 points

Always: ☐ 5 points

Points Received: ......3..........

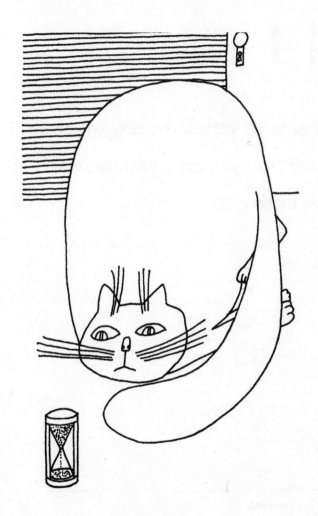

41

14

Is able to watch moving objects with his eyes only, without moving his body

(is aware of movement but keeps body rigid and still).

Never: ☑ 1 point

Seldom: ☐ 2 points

Often: ☐ 3 points

Usually: ☐ 4 points

Always: ☐ 5 points

Points Received: ....

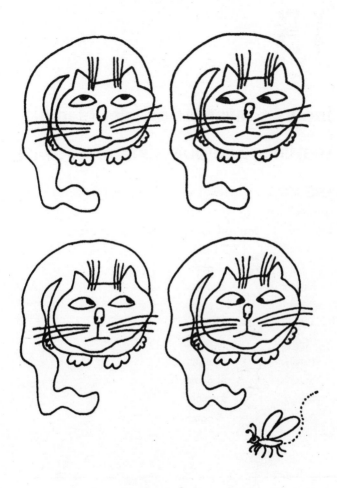

15

Shows awareness of odours in his immediate surroundings

(either likes or dislikes the smell of perfumes, lotions, medicines, foods, animals, etc.).

Never: ☑ 1 point

Seldom: ☐ 2 points

Often: ☐ 3 points

Usually: ☐ 4 points

Always: ☐ 5 points

Points Received: ....

45

16

Makes various sounds to request different needs

(specific cries for hunger, injury, pain, attention, pleasure, etc.).

Never: ☐ 1 point

Seldom: ☐ 2 points

Often: ☐ 3 points

Usually: ☐ 4 points

Always: ☑ 5 points

Points Received: ......5......

47

17

Shows or displays his feelings toward other animals or people in his household

(e.g. jealousy, love, worry).

Never:	☐	1 point
Seldom:	☑	2 points
Often:	☐	3 points
Usually:	☐	4 points
Always:	☐	5 points

Points Received: ......2..........

18

Has preference for certain animals

(e.g. plays with certain animals, enjoys the presence of other animals, likes to watch animals on television).

Never: ☐ 1 point

Seldom: ☐ 2 points

Often: ☐ 3 points

Usually: ☐ 4 points

Always: ☐ 5 points

Points Received: 4

19

Favours one front paw over the other and uses this favourite paw for various activities

(e.g. washing face, playing with toys, grasping objects).

Never:	☑	1 point
Seldom:	☐	2 points
Often:	☐	3 points
Usually:	☐	4 points
Always:	☐	5 points

Points Received: ...1...............

20

Shows preference for specific objects

(e.g. favourite pillow, toy, blanket).

Never: ☐ 1 point

Seldom: ☐ 2 points

Often: ☐ 3 points

Usually: ☐ 4 points

Always: ☑ 5 points

Points Received: 5

21

Enjoys being touched around neck, face and back

(especially stroking or petting).

Never:	☐	1 point
Seldom:	☐	2 points
Often:	☐	3 points
Usually:	☐	4 points
Always:	☑	5 points

Points Received: 5.................

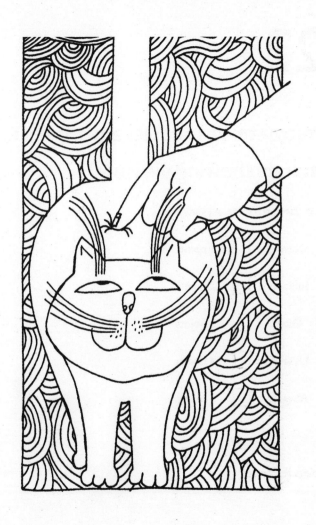

22

Sits on or near adults and makes sounds showing pleasure

(e.g. purring, cooing, gurgling).

Never: ☐   1 point

Seldom: ☐   2 points

Often: ☐   3 points

Usually: ☑   4 points

Always: ☐   5 points

Points Received: 4

23

Reacts to music and rhythm

(e.g. sitting on radio or piano, moving in time to the music by rocking, dancing, twitching tail).

Never:	☐	1 point
Seldom:	☐	2 points
Often:	☐	3 points
Usually:	☑	4 points
Always:	☐	5 points

Points Received: ...4...

24

Is aware of the passing of time

(e.g. can predict or anticipate when certain people will return home, or leave home).

Never: ☑ I point

Seldom: ☐ 2 points

Often: ☐ 3 points

Usually: ☐ 4 points

Always: ☐ 5 points

Points Received: ....

25

Can predict change in the weather that will take place within one week

(e.g. hides before storm comes, stays close to fireplace before severe cold arrives, seems to know when unusual weather is approaching).

Never: ☑ 1 point

Seldom: ☐ 2 points

Often: ☐ 3 points

Usually: ☐ 4 points

Always: ☐ 5 points

Points Received: ...1...........

TOTAL POINTS SECTION A:...85.........

Section B: Cat Performance Test

Materials Needed

1. Shoestring or thick yarn, approximately 30 inches long.
2. Small ball made of plastic, wood or rubber.
3. Pencil (use eraser end or an unsharpened pencil).
4. Feather or thick rubber band.
5. Bell, or butter knife and small drinking glass.

Directions

Gather the testing materials needed, then perform each of the activities up to five times to obtain the best possible response. Section B usually takes about 15 minutes. Before administering the test, make sure your cat is calm, co-operative and in a good mood. If he become tired, disinterested, nervous or uncooperative, or leaves the testing area, this part of the test should be stopped until the cat is more comfortable.

Recording

Make a tick next to each response given by your pet. Performance items may have more than one tick. Some performances items may have no ticks.

Scoring

Add up the total number of points earned and record this total at the end of Section B. No credit is given if the pet continually runs away or refuses to respond.

I

Touch or stroke your cat lightly and gently around the mouth area with your finger.

Closes eyes: ☑ 2 points

Shakes head: ☐ 2 points

Licks mouth: ☐ 4 points

Credit Points: .....2.....

2

Touch your cat gently on his back with your finger or the pencil.

Ripples or moves back fur: ☐ 2 points

Shakes fur: ☑ 2 points

Licks spot touched: ☐ 4 points

Credit Points: ....2....

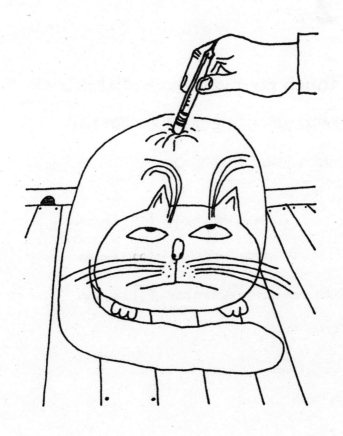

3

Touch the inside hair of either
of your cat's ears very lightly
with your finger or pencil.

Shakes entire head:	☐	2 points
Twitched the ear:	✓☑4	4 points
Rubs or touches the ear with paw:	☐	4 points

Credit Points: ...4...........

4

Ring the bell or tap a glass with a butter knife to make a soft ringing noise behind your cat.

Moves or twitches ear(s):	☐	2 points
Turns head partly around:	☐	2 points
Turns head completely around to the area where the sound came from:	☑	4 points

Credit Points: 4

5

Place the string or yarn on your cat's back. Be careful not to let the string hang down and touch the floor. Completely let go of string.

Ripples or moves fur: ☐ 2 points

Removes string in any way: ☑ 4 points

Credit Points: ...4...........

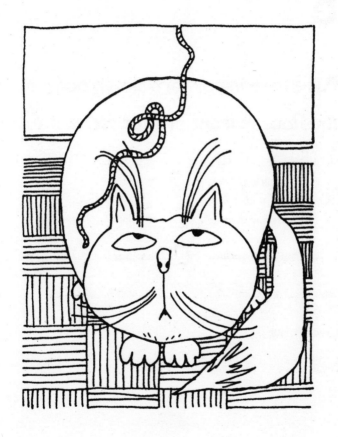

6

Pull the string or yarn slowly across
the floor in front of your cat.

Watched with eyes:	☐	2 points
Touches with nose:	☐	2 points
Grabs with paw(s):	☑	4 points

Credit Points: ....4.......

7

Place the feather or thick rubber band on the floor two to four inches in front of your cat.

Touches with paw(s):	☐	2 points
Touches with nose:	☐	2 points
Begins to chew feather or rubber band:	☐	2 points
Picks up feather or rubber band with paw(s):	☐	4 points
Transfers feather or rubber band between paws:	☑	4 points

Credit Points: ....4........

8

Slowly move the pencil along the
floor toward your cat.

Touches pencil with paw: ☐ 2 points

Touches pencil with same
paw two or more times: ☑ 4 points

Credit Points: ....4.........

9

Roll the ball on the floor towards your cat.

Touches with paw:	☐	2 points
Touches with nose:	☐	2 points
Begins to play with ball:	☑	4 points

Credit Points: ...4...........

TOTAL POINTS SECTION B: ...32...

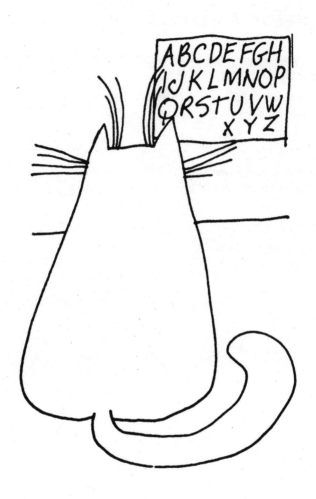

Section C: Extra Credit

Directions

Read each of the following statements to determine if your pet qualifies for these bonus points.

Recording

Enter the number of bonus points earned to the right of each item. Partial credit is not permitted.

Scoring

At the end of Section C, add up the total number of points your pet has received.

I

Is able to make sounds *upon request.*

Qualifies: ☑   4 bonus points

Points Earned: ....4........

2

Can sit, stand, or roll over *upon request.*

Qualifies: ☑ 4 bonus points

Points Earned: ...4...........

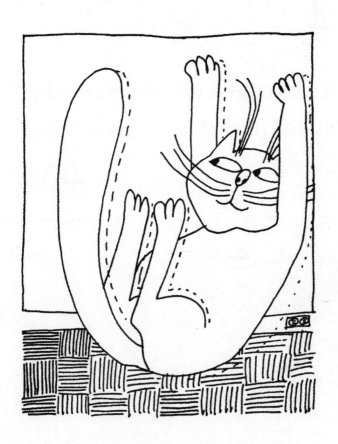

3

Is able to pass any item from paw to paw or hit it back and forth in the air.

Qualifies: ☐ 4 bonus points

Points Earned: ...○...........

4

Has learned to use the people's toilet instead of a litter box.

Qualifies: ☐ 4 bonus points

Points Earned: 6

5

Is able to balance on hind legs for at least five seconds.

Qualifies: ☑   4 bonus points

Points Earned: ...4...........

6

Has learned to walk on hind legs for at least five steps.

Qualifies: ☑ 4 bonus points

Points Earned: ....4..........

**TOTAL NUMBER
OF BONUS POINTS:** ...16..........

Section D: Credit Deductions

Directions

Read each of the following statements to determine if points should be taken away from your cat's score.

Recording

Place the number of deducted points to the right of each item.

Scoring

Add up the total number of point deductions. Record this total at the end of Section D.

I

Continually runs into walls or doors.

Qualifies: ☐ deduct I point

Points Taken Away: ..6..............

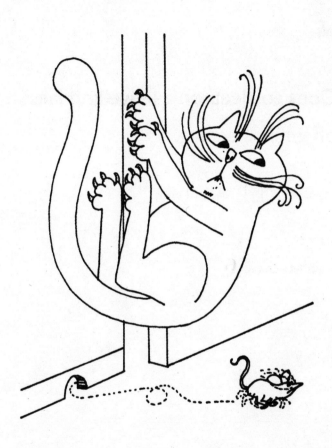

2

Goes to sleep on a ledge and falls off while sleeping.

Qualifies: ☐   deduct 1 point

Points Taken Away: 0 ....

3

Constantly sits, stands, steps or
sleeps in his food dish.

Qualifies: ☐ deduct I point

Points Taken Away: 0 ....

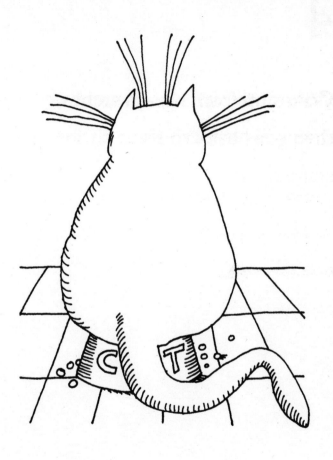

4

Wakes up from nap, stretches, then goes back to sleep sitting or standing up.

Qualifies: ☐ deduct 1 point

Points Taken Away: 0...............

5

Goes to sleep in closet or drawer
and ends up trapped inside.

Qualifies: ☐ deduct 1 point

Points Taken Away: ...0.............

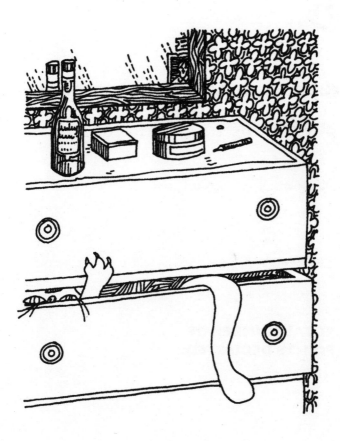

6

Jumps onto toilet when seat is up and falls in.

Qualifies: ☐ deduct 1 point

Points Taken Away: 0 ....

TOTAL NUMBER OF POINTS DEDUCTED: 0 ....

Scoring the Cat IQ Test

Step 1

Add together the number of points earned in Sections A, B and C.

Section A = 85 ....points
Section B = 32 ....points
Section C = 12 ....points

   Total = 129 ....

Step 2

Subtract any points listed in Section D.

Section D = 0 ....points to subtract

Total Test Score: [A + B + C] – D = 133 ....

Step 3

Use this Total Test Score when referring to the Cat IQ Classification Chart overleaf. Now you can know how smart your cat is – really!

Cat IQ Classification Chart

Total Test Score	Classification
60–69	Below Normal
70–89	Low Normal
90–109	Normal
110–119	Above Normal
120–139	Superior
140 and above	Genius

Analysing Your Cat's Performance

Your cat's score on The Cat IQ Test should give you some idea of his intellectual development at the present time. It will also give you an idea of how your cat's learning skills and understanding ability compare to those of other cats. Many factors influence this score, such as the cat's age, background, and experience. A young kitten, for example, may score better as it matures. Other factors are in your control, and later on there will be some suggestions on how you can improve your cat's performance.

This section will provide you with definitions of each of the categories on the Classification Chart. By reading about your cat's category, you will gain a greater understanding of your cat's abilities and needs.

Genius Range

Cats with a score of 140 or more are gifted and extremely bright. They are able to function well socially and exhibit exceptional reasoning skills. Extremely well developed co-ordination and balance have been demonstrated. They communicate well and often develop strong and distinct relationships with their owners. Without a doubt, these cats are quite creative and original in the ways they cope with their daily lives. These pets are often very attractive, mature, healthy and stable.

Superior Range

Pets that are grouped within the 120 to 139 point range are usually quite clever and able to grasp new information quickly. These pets are highly intelligent and easily gain the attention and approval of their owners. Pets within this category are well co-ordinated and have good muscle development and posture. They are usually mature and can adjust quickly to changing situations. They have learned to get along smoothly with their owners and family and have mastered the skills they need to survive.

Above Normal Range

Cats that scored between 110 and 119 points have demonstrated good intellectual ability. These pets display common sense, strong social skills and a better than average ability to communicate. Cats that fall within this range are co-operative and friendly, physically well developed and able to cope with most frustrations.

Normal Range

Cats that are grouped within the 90 to 109 point range are well liked by their owners and are able to cope with the usual demands made upon them. A sufficient amount of communication between pet and owner exists for a good relationship. Co-ordination is also satisfactory. These cats are sociable and have developed adequate ways of coping with life's daily frustrations.

Low Normal Range

Cats whose scores fall within the 70 to 89 point range may need extra time or experience to realise their potential. These pets are usually friendly and tend to be adjusted to their surroundings. They are able to function quite well in spite of possible minor weaknesses in communication, co-ordination or social behaviour. These pets often improve their scores when they are older or more mature.

Below Normal Range

Pets that are classified in the 60 to 69 point range appear to be in need of special assistance; otherwise, they may encounter some difficulties coping with their daily routine. Lack of experience, lack of attention or lack of the right type of surroundings may have contributed to their weak performances. Additional time and care will often lead to considerable improvement.

How to Improve Your Cat's IQ

Your cat's score on The Cat IQ Test is not just the result of his own abilities. Many factors influence his performance: his age, his background and his experience, for example. Some of these factors are in your control. The following techniques should increase your cat's intelligence and happiness, regardless of how well he did on the test.

1. Encourage your cat's natural (and infinite) curiosity. Present your pet with new and novel toys and equipment and even food (though don't overfeed him). Praise your cat for his attempts to approach new things.
2. Set aside a specific amount of time each day to talk and play with your pet. If you spark his interest, even the most sober cat can become as playful as he was as a kitten,
3. Keep your voice pleasing and comforting. Cats respond quickly to the voice level of those around them.
4. Reward your cat immediately for good behaviour. Do not delay, as this will confuse him. Rewards such as a favourite toy, special food or a gentle petting may be given.
5. Promote a healthy and stable relationship with your pet through physical contact such as brushing, combing or rubbing your cat daily. This will help develop and promote feelings of security and foster a high level of emotional stability.

6. Make your pet feel important and needed by praising him for the things he does well. Provide opportunities for him to repeat that activity and encourage him to do so. Don't frustrate your cat by demanding or expecting him to do things he can't.

7. Be consistent when enforcing rules of conduct. Make sure your cat knows what type of behaviour is expected from him. If he consistently behaves incorrectly in certain situations, set up a mock situation to provoke the behaviour (for example, set the table for dinner and wait for your cat to jump up) and then discipline the cat immediately. Punishment should always be immediate and firm, but gentle.

8. Eliminate the teasing or tormenting situations your pet encounters. Make sure that children know not to pull a cat's tail, for example. Try to provide only a minimal amount of physical and emotional stress.

9. Be sensitive to the needs of your cat. However, do not let him manipulate you. A relationship of mutual trust and admiration is necessary to foster both intelligence and happiness.

Comparative Scores by Age, Sex and Type

The tables on the following pages compare the performances of cats of various ages, sexes and general types.

Table A depicts the predicted distribution of scores if every cat in the cat population were to take the test. The scores in tables B, C and D are based only on a limited and biased sampling of cats. This included only cats held in high esteem by their owners and did not include any neglected, unwanted, homeless or sick cats. As a result, the scores on tables B, C and D are significantly higher than they would be if they were based on a random sampling of cats, and no definite conclusions should be drawn from these comparative tables. We do hope, however, that this section provides you with a context for rating your cat's intelligence, as well as being a starting point for future studies.

Table A

Predicted Distribution of Scores for All Cats

Classification Category	Percentage Predicted (%)
Below Normal Range	2.20
Low Normal Range	14.15
Normal Range	68.30
Above Normal Range	14.18
Superior Range	2.15
Genius Range	0.02

Table B

Scores by Age

Age*	Mean Score
8 months to 3 years	108
4 years to 7 years	133
8 years to 11 years	144
12 years to 15 years	123

* Age should have little influence on the intellectual development of cats, except in the case of a very young, immature or highly distracted kitten. Once again, these results are based only on a limited and biased sample.

Table C

Scores by Sex

Sex*	Mean Score†
Male	140.00
Female	117.25

* Neutered cats were included in the sampling.

† The superior scores of male cats here can be attributed to the high percentage of Siamese males among the male cats tested. This breed scored significantly better than others on the test (see Table D). Since the breed factor corrupted the sex factor here, no definite conclusions about the relative intelligence of male and female cats should be drawn from this sampling.

Table D

Scores by Type

General Type*	Mean Score†
Long-haired	121.5
Short-haired	122
Siamese	140

* These three general types of cats were listed here, rather than specific breeds, because of the limited number of cats or certain breeds in the norming sample.

† The difference in the scores of long-haired and short-haired cats is not statistically significant. However, Siamese cats did score significantly higher than other types. This can be attributed to the superior communication skills evident in that breed. Siamese cats are often very vocal and expressive.

Scorecard

This answer sheet may be photocopied and used instead of recording the results in the book.

Section A (Observation Scale)

1. ...... 6. ...... 11. ...... 16. ...... 21. ......

2. ...... 7. ...... 12. ...... 17. ...... 22. ......

3. ...... 8. ...... 13. ...... 18. ...... 23. ......

4. ...... 9. ...... 14. ...... 19. ...... 24. ......

5. ...... 10. ...... 15. ...... 20. ...... 25. ...... Total = ...

Section B (Performance Scale)

1. ...... 4. ...... 7. ......

2. ...... 5. ...... 8. ......

3. ...... 6. ...... 9. ...... Total = ...

Section C (Extra Credit)

1. ...... 3. ...... 5. ......

2. ...... 4. ...... 6. ...... Total = ...

Section D (Deductions)

1. ...... 3. ...... 5. ......

2. ...... 4. ...... 6. ...... Total = ...

SCORING: A + B + C – D =

TOTAL TEST SCORE: ....

Certificate of Merit

This certifies that

_____

has participated in an assessment of intellectual ability and is awarded this certificate of merit for completion of

The Cat IQ Test

Date

Examiner's Signature